GOD IS MOVING

MOVING

Who Will Follow?

1998 International Mission Study for Adults

by Erich Bridges

About the Author

Erich Bridges has been a writer and editor for the
Southern Baptist International Mission Board since 1981.
His reporting on missions work around the world has
taken him to 16 countries, and he has written hundreds of
articles for Baptist Press, *The Commission* magazine, and
many other publications. He also authored the 1987 Adult
International Mission Study, *The Land of Morning Prayer*,
about South Korea.

Erich and his wife, Hwa Chong, are members of Grace
Community Baptist Church in Richmond, Virginia. They
have two children, Joshua and Heather.

Woman's Missionary Union
P. O. Box 830010
Birmingham, AL 35283-0010

Dewey Decimal Classification: 266.023
Subject Headings: Missions, International Missions

Verses in this work are taken from *The Living Bible*, copyright © 1971
by Tyndale House Publishers, Wheaton, IL. Used by permission.

ISBN: 1-56309-264-6

W984113•0498•12M1

Contents

Overview
World-Shaking Change,
Wonder-Working Power

Change and power. As the world approaches the end of the 20th century—and the second millennium after Christ—change is everywhere, for better or worse. However, few leaders know where real power lies.

This is the century in which fools, professing to be wise, declared God dead. That conclusion opened the door for men like Soviet dictator, Joseph Stalin. He thought power lay in the barrel of a gun. Stalin and his many imitators swallowed nations and peoples whole and tried to bury Christianity.

Less then 40 years after Stalin's death, Soviet communism has lost most of its power and suffers under the accusations of people long oppressed.

Yet democracy is also a fallible human institution, not a divine one. It has failed time and again to fulfill the deepest hopes human beings have invested in it. As our century draws to a close, a certain weariness and disillusionment permeate many societies. The West won the Cold War, we are told. So why isn't everyone happy? Like the elderly Solomon in Ecclesiastes reflecting on all he has seen, we have realized the vanity of our arrogance.

The border crossing gate between East and West Berlin

The wall surrounding West Berlin

Communism sought for much of the century to destroy the church, or silence it with tyranny and terror. In the West, powerful forces of materialism, secularism, and relativism—hostile to faith or any absolute—have relentlessly mocked Christianity and attempted to drive Christians from the public marketplace of ideas.

These philosophies exalt humanity over God. The result: chaos, emptiness, and despair. Exhibit A: the United States, where a cultural civil war has raged for decades. That war may yet destroy us as a society, with faith and every other value that once held us together still under attack.

Yet just as Christianity seems to be fighting for survival in its old bastions of Europe and America, the gospel is marching through doors that are opening after decades or centuries. Communism worldwide isn't dead just yet. But as it gasps for breath, missionaries and local believers are spreading the good news of Christ all over the old communist world. Marx, Lenin, Stalin, and Mao lie in their tombs, but Jesus is alive!

As nations created by politicians and armies crumble, Christians have realized anew that the ethnic people groups who make up those nations are far older and more durable.

These are the same ethnae—translated *nations* in the English Bible—that Jesus commands us to disciple in the Great Commission of Matthew 28:18–20. More and more missionaries are putting their efforts into evangelizing the most unreached of these people groups. New believers are being baptized in places once thought beyond the reach of the gospel.

Mission strategists across the evangelical spectrum now agree that—despite all the internal and external challenges we face—Christians can carry the gospel farther and wider than ever before.

Once symbols of communist oppression, the Berlin Wall and the border crossings are now memories, reminding us of the startling changes taking place in our world today.

Cause for Celebration

When missionary William Carey, known as the father of modern missions, left England for India more than 200 years ago, "evangelical Christianity had only penetrated a handful of the . . . people (groups) outside Europe and eastern North America," observes missions strategist Patrick Johnstone, author of *Operation World*.

Today, by contrast, Christian disciples among thousands of people groups have the gospel resources to reach their own people. "What a change!" Johnstone rejoices.

What a change, indeed. And Southern Baptists have played a key role in bringing it about—by expecting great things from God and attempting great things for Him. More than 13,000 Southern Baptist missionaries have followed Carey overseas in the century and a half since the Southern Baptist Convention—and its mission boards—were formed in 1845 "for the purpose of . . . eliciting, combining and directing the energies of the whole denomination in one sacred effort, for the propagation of the Gospel. . . ."[1]

Exactly 150 years later, International Mission Board leaders restated the mission this way: "We will lead Southern Baptists to be on mission with God to bring all the peoples of the world to saving faith in Jesus Christ."

Nearly 4,300 Southern Baptist missionaries were at work around the world in 1997, with more than 17,000 short-term volunteers serving alongside them. Southern Baptists helped start 2,451 churches with local Christians, and baptized 283,100 new believers in Christ.

Even more exciting, many of those churches were started and those believers were baptized in "The Last Frontier"—so named by mission strategists because it is largely cut off from traditional missions. Up to 1.3 billion people live in areas denied access to the Christian gospel by hostile cultures, religions, and governments. Many live in the Muslim world of north Africa, the Mideast, and Asia.

"Just a few years ago, the idea of sowing, watering, and harvesting in such places seemed as remote for Southern Baptists as the places themselves," says Southern Baptist International Mission Board President, Jerry Rankin.

"But viewing the world as God does shows its people in a whole new light. The boundaries between nations, drawn during conferences of world powers during the late 19th century, begin to blur. Distinct ethno-linguistic groups come into focus. Over 6,000 of these unreached ethno-linguistic groups exist. Easily one third of them have never heard the good news of Jesus Christ, nor had the opportunity to respond to the gospel in their own language.

"By placing one missionary couple with each group, Southern Baptists could bring a witness to these unreached groups of The Last Frontier. But we would have to double the number of workers now serving through the International Mission Board. The harvest is truly plentiful, but the workers are few."

There is reason for optimism, however. Of The Last Frontier's 187 strategic *megapeoples*—those with more than one million people each—Southern Baptists now minister in more than 125.

God's Mission, Not Ours

This is God's mission, not our own. As Avery Willis, senior vice president of the International Mission Board, wrote in his book, *The Biblical Basis of Missions*:

> Missions originated in the heart of God. It is not something we decide to do for God, but God reveals His purpose to us so that we may have a creative part in His mission. Make no mistake, we do not initiate the mission nor will we consummate it. But somehow, some way, and to some extent, God has limited what He will do. That limit is the possibility of what He can do through us.

> Today the church has the God-given missionary

assignment, once entrusted to Israel, to preach to all the nations. This task, this privilege, belongs to every Christian—not just those in vocational ministry, not just missionaries, not just the most gifted. The ways we participate—through prayer, volunteer service, short-term or career missionary service, or financial support—may vary, but the task is for all.

Often, explains Willis, "missions is perceived as a super special assignment for extraordinary people. Nothing could be further from God's purpose. . . . God's purpose is to use ordinary people who believe in and serve an extraordinary God."

This mission study looks at the world through the eyes of six such people:

Charles and Phyllis Hardie live the love of Christ in Siberia.

• Charles and Phyllis Hardie: A Southern Baptist missionary couple with nearly two decades of service in Taiwan, they could have completed their careers in a place where they were comfortable and fruitful. Instead, they responded to a call from the International Mission Board for veteran missionaries to step through the doors opened by the collapse of the Soviet Union. That act of obedience took the Hardies to a forbidding place indeed—Siberia.

• Dewey and Bobbie Dunn: Since they became involved in volunteer medical missions in the '80s, the Dunns have helped bring more souls into God's kingdom than many career missionaries. For the Dunns, missions is more than a sermon topic or an occasional trip. It is a passion and a life purpose that they have spread to hundreds of other Southern Baptist health professionals drawn to volunteer service by the Dunns' contagious enthusiasm.

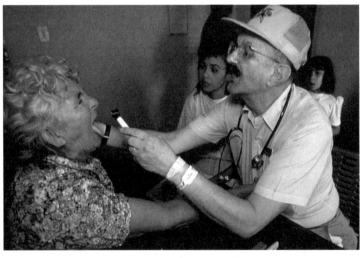

Dr. Dewey Dunn demonstrates the love of Christ by his actions.

• Troy and Melissa Haas: Just being on the missions field wasn't enough for this adventurous young missionary couple. Like the Apostle Paul, Troy and Melissa aspired to preach Christ where His name had never been heard before—among the Turkana people in far northwestern Kenya. With their daughter, Rachel, they live in a thatched hut. Once they master the Turkana language, they plan to travel with this nomadic people.

Melissa and Rachel Haas are transplants for Christ among the
nomadic tribes of the Turkana in Kenya.

Radical Christians, Radical Churches

To accomplish His objective in the probable world of the
21st century—a world even more convulsed by change
and turmoil than our own—God needs more people like
the Hardies, the Dunns, and the Haases. He needs Southern Baptist young people, college students, seminarians,
volunteers, short-term workers, and career missionaries
with the characteristics of "frontiersmen"—and women:

- Fierce independence
- Challenged by the great unknown
- Able to innovate
- Willing to take risks for long-term gain

There's no time to waste. The world needs 200,000
new missionaries now, declares George Verwer, a leader in
the A.D. 2000 and Beyond movement. Despite the exciting growth in the number of missionaries emerging from
countries that once were missions fields, he believes half of
these new workers should come from the United States.

Yet Western evangelical missionary ranks are shrinking, not growing. As recently as a decade ago, 50,000 career missionaries came from America alone. But that number reportedly plummeted to 41,000 within five years. As post-World War II missionaries have retired, not enough members of younger generations have stepped forward to take their place.

In the past, we assumed denominational missions ranked high in Southern Baptist churches. A study prepared for the International Mission Board concluded that assumption is no longer valid. It found that the churches surveyed "tended to be more inwardly focused, more concerned with their congregations . . . than with foreign missions." Churches were aware of missions activities, but were "not overly enthusiastic" about them.

But there's encouraging evidence that many young missionary candidates are counteracting such trends.

"They feel drawn to the cutting edge," says Lloyd Atkinson, who oversees missions personnel selection for the International Mission Board. "They want to go places where there are no other missionaries and life is hard. They want to go where the need is the greatest—even into dangerous, uncharted waters.

"This is a significant, encouraging trend. God is calling people to these new opportunities, and we can look at their lives and see how God has prepared them. That says to me that God knew a long time ago these doors would open, and He began preparing them to serve."

We need radical Christians and radical churches for the 21st century—radical in their obedience to fulfilling God's mission. That is actually normal from God's perspective, but it looks radical to the world, and even to other Christians.

How does the typical Christian—or church—become a radical one? Simply by obeying God, and following in Christ's footsteps.

As John Stott writes: "Christian mission is rooted in the nature of God himself. The Bible reveals him as a missionary God (Father, Son and Holy Spirit), who creates a missionary people and is working towards a missionary consummation. . . . Now (Christ) sends us into the world, as the Father sent him into the world."

Missions is not a program or a budget item to be inserted somewhere (usually near the bottom) on a long menu of ministry options for local churches. Missions is our reason for being in this world; missions is God's work through us until He returns, as Paul writes in 2 Corinthians 5:18–20:

"All these new things are from God who brought us back to Himself through what Jesus Christ did. And God has given us the privilege of urging everyone to come into his favor and be reconciled to him. For God was in Christ, restoring the world to himself, no longer counting men's sins against them but blotting them out. This is the wonderful message he has given us to tell others. We are Christ's ambassadors. God is using us to speak to you."

Many Christians today ask, "Why should I be involved in missions?" In light of God's perspective as revealed in the Bible, His response might be, "Why should you be involved in anything else?"

Until we join God in His task, we are modern-day Jonahs—disobedient and useless to Him—and modern-day Ninevahs remain lost in darkness.

If we do join Him, He will shake the world through us—by His wonder-working power!

[1] *Taken from the convention constitution's preamble.*

By giving to the Lottie Moon Christmas Offering and the Cooperative Program, you support the work of God through missionaries like the Hardies and the Haases. Even if you don't feel called to full-time missions, you may wish to give of your time in volunteer service. Volunteers, such as the Dunns, pay their own expenses. If you wish to volunteer in international missions, call 1-800-888-8657 for more information.

Voluntary Exile

Charles and Phyllis Hardie in Siberia

In a place once infamous for imprisonment and death, Russians are finding freedom and life in Jesus—thanks to a missionary couple's willing 'exile'.

Siberia. Land of bitter cold. Land of bitter exile.

Russia's communist rulers sent many of their enemies—both real and imagined—there, along with countless innocent victims of the Soviet state: political prisoners, ethnic minorities, and Christians.

Torn from their homes and families, millions arrived in Siberia to face hard labor, imprisonment, often death. Countless bodies remain frozen beneath the permafrost in the places where they died from hunger, cold, or a bullet in the head.

Communist tyranny may be history in Russia, at least for now. But even today, who would willingly go to this frigid place so full of the ghosts of memory?

Southern Baptist missionaries Charles and Phyllis Hardie would, and did. Going there—and staying there—is the toughest thing they've ever done, but several new and growing congregations of Siberian Christians are thankful they did.

Why did the Hardies go into "voluntary exile" in Siberia? Rewind to the early '90s.

Vast portions of the rusted Iron Curtain erected by the communists around Russia and Eastern Europe are finally creaking open—or falling down altogether—after seven long decades. Soviet rule is crumbling. The Soviet state itself ceases to exist in 1992 as nations held prisoner for generations regain their independence.

And for the first time in generations, Baptists and other Christians are allowed to invite evangelical missionaries to come and help them heal the wounds of the past and proclaim God's light in lands long dominated by darkness.

The call goes out among Southern

The Kremlin in Moscow, once the seat of government for the Soviet Union, is now the seat of the Russian government.

Baptists, who have long prayed for their oppressed brethren in Russia and Eastern Europe. The Foreign (now International) Mission Board hurries to mobilize missionaries to enter a host of once-closed fields. Not just new missionaries, either.

No one knows how long the door will stay open. So mission strategists call on veteran missionaries serving on other fields to consider moving into post-communist Russia and Europe—as quickly as possible—to "set the table" for new missionaries and volunteers who will follow. Veterans already accustomed to life and work overseas can adjust to a new culture more quickly (in theory, at least), and become effective ministers in a short time.

The Long Arm of the Call

The call for help reached all the way to Charles and Phyllis Hardie, who were nearing the end of their second decade of mission service in Taiwan.

Appointed missionaries in 1974, the Hardies—he's from Alabama, she's from Georgia—had been busy ever since in the city of Taichung, home to more than a million people. They had taught, started churches, led many students to the Lord, discipled new believers—and won the

Worshipping in the Moscow Baptist Church

affection and deep respect of their Chinese and missionary colleagues.

"They learned early the importance of hospitality and making their home available to people," observes retired missionary Jack Gentry, one of Charles' closest friends and coworkers in Taiwan. "Their most striking characteristic is their willingness to invest deeply in the lives of individuals and families."

The Hardies complement each other, both in personality and as ministry partners. Charles is quiet, devoted to Scripture memory, and a master at one-on-one discipleship. Phyllis is talkative and outgoing. She excels in one-on-one relationships too, but also loves groups, being a hostess, and cooking for a crowd—the larger the better.

As the '90s began, the Hardies looked forward to another fruitful decade of ministry in Taichung. They went on a US furlough in 1992 fully expecting to return to Taiwan.

"We were going to be teaching English, reaching students, and church-planting at the new Chiang Kai-shek University," says Charles. "We'd have a new car and a new apartment. We could go once a week to where we had ministered before to pray with the missionaries we had known for 20 years. We could buy our food at the American supermarket. We had everything lined out."

Or so they thought.

During the furlough, they began to feel a sense of spiritual restlessness. The last of their three daughters had left home for college in 1990. The nest was empty—a bittersweet time for the Hardies as parents but also a time of new flexibility for them as missionaries. World-shaking changes were occurring in the Soviet Union and its former satellites. The Foreign Mission Board was asking missionaries on other fields to consider transferring to Russia or Eastern Europe to spread the gospel while the opportunity was ripe.

"We were experienced missionaries, and the [Berlin] Wall had come down, and there were new doors opening," Charles remembers. "I said to my boss [Sam James, then-vice president for Southern Baptist missions work in Asia] in passing, 'If you have something in that part of the world, we'd be willing to look into it.' He gave me 10 places to pray about in Russia, and said there was a real need in Novosibirsk"—the biggest city in Siberia.

Charles retreated to a quiet place for five days of fasting and prayer: "I simply asked the Lord, *What would You have us do?* God put it all together."

The decision didn't come completely out of the blue. Charles had been praying for years about using his Chinese language skills to minister—perhaps as an English teacher—in communist China.

But after paying their dues over many years to learn a new culture and a difficult language, who could have blamed the Hardies if they had finished their missionary career in comfortable roles in modern, urban Taiwan? Phyllis answers, "This has always been my heart cry: *Where are there people who have not had a chance to hear the gospel of Jesus?* In Taiwan, lots of people have never heard, but they have had the opportunity to hear. If you are seeking to know the Lord in Taiwan, you can find the Lord, because there are more churches. But Siberia was closed

Downtown Novosibirsk

for over 70 years."

That didn't make it any easier to say goodbye to dear friends in Taiwan. Before heading for Russia, the Hardies returned one last time to their long-time missions field to pack their belongings, bid farewell, and shed many tears.

Siberia

On June 30, 1993, the Hardies arrived in Novosibirsk after a 2,250-mile journey by train from Moscow across Russia's vastness. The remote Siberian city of two million souls is much closer to Mongolia and China than to Russia's capital.

At the train station in Novosibirsk, local Baptists awaited the missionary couple with flowers and a warm welcome. "They have finally sent us real Baptist missionaries!" pastor Eduard Genrich exulted. Even the weather was warm; Novosibirsk actually gets quite hot during the short summer.

Church members drove them through the city's wide avenues, across the Obb River, and into a seemingly endless procession of identical gray high-rise apartment buildings—the typical face of Soviet architecture.

Novosibirsk . . . an endless skyline of identical gray high-rise apartment buildings

They shared their first tiny, two-bedroom apartment with a young Russian couple. It had a kitchen and bath, but no telephone, washer, or dryer. Phyllis washed their clothes by hand and hung them over the water pipes in the bathroom. Before the end of the year they would find another apartment (with a phone) of their own.

After the initial round of introductions and welcomes

from the city's three Baptist churches, Charles and Phyllis began the slow, painstaking daily task of learning to speak Russian, finding stores where they could buy food and other essentials, and preparing for their first Siberian winter.

"Cold, cold, and colder," is how one missionary colleague describes what they faced that winter. Temperatures regularly sank as low as 45 degrees below zero—before factoring in wind chill. The Hardies huddled in their flat with three and four layers of outer clothing, coats, and an ancient hot-water radiator.

"Even though we have double windows and our outside walls are 32 inches thick, you still feel that cold air from the window," says Charles. "But you prepare for it and it just becomes part of life." Preparation is the key word, especially for going outside, where waiting for a tardy bus results in numbness in the extremities and can cause frostbite.

The Southern Baptist missions organization supplied them with two space heaters, which made the apartment a little cozier. But a Russian couple with four children—and no heat at all—asked to borrow the heaters.

"Of course we couldn't say no," Phyllis says. "We haven't had the heart to ask for them back because they are now dear friends. I couldn't live with myself if their children were cold and we were selfishly taking them back just to be a little more comfortable."

Harder to bear than the frigid air was the initial loneliness—especially for Phyllis.

"In that (first) apartment we felt very isolated," Phyllis recalls. "We had no phone. We couldn't communicate with anyone. We had no friends in the city. We had each other and we had the Lord."

During those early days, several Baptist families went out of their way to love the American newcomers in ways the Hardies remain grateful for: invitations to homes and meals, special help with translation and language struggles, encouraging words, and prayers.

Once the Hardies got their bearings, of course, friendships began to bloom everywhere. A translator would

Charles Hardie studies Russian.

introduce a friend, who would introduce another friend, setting the stage for small Bible studies. Charles also began an evangelistic Bible study with mainland Chinese students studying in Novosibirsk.

"I got to know my neighbor right off the bat because she had a grandson that was living with her," Phyllis relates. "She would come over and say, 'Phyllis, they have sugar at such and such a place but you need to go right now and get it.' Because we have lived there among them, we've had several times where they have sent people to us who wanted to ask questions about God."

One night, the woman who managed their entire block of apartment buildings visited and asked for a Bible. They gave her one. Soon she returned and asked for a simpler version for her grandson. They gave her a children's Bible. Before she left, she said, "I haven't finished reading the Bible you gave me. Could I keep it a few more days?"

"It's yours; it's a gift," Phyllis told her.

The woman came a third time and said, "We still haven't finished reading it. Can we please keep it longer?" Charles emphasized once again that it was a gift.

"I think she finally realized we were serious," Phyllis

recalls. "That we were living among them, that we weren't a cult, that we were genuine people, that we were loving because of Jesus loving us."

The Hardies' early isolation was further allayed by the arrival of three Southern Baptist coworkers: missionary journeymen Devita Bussell and Todd Nance, and International Service Corps worker Greg Whitehead. The Hardies took the young two-year workers under their wing and helped them reach out to young Russians. "They treated us like their own kids from the start," says Todd. "We really enjoyed that."

"We were a team. We worked together. We planned together. We prayed together," says Phyllis. "We ate together at least once a week, and they had keys to our apartment and came in and out whenever they wanted to. We were their home base. They were a great encouragement to us because they carried this load with us."

Reach Out or Not?

But then something disturbing happened that would prove far more difficult for the Hardies than the cold or isolation of Novosibirsk: The Siberian Baptist leaders, particularly the older ones, strongly warned them not to make friends outside the church or to invite non-Baptists into their home.

The admonition went against the Hardies' personalities and natural ministry gifts. It also directly conflicted with one of their main missions assignments: to reach out to young and middle-aged couples and singles with the aim of starting churches among people basically untouched by the gospel. This is Russia's "lost generation"—people raised in a time when communism was already dead in spirit if not in fact, people searching for something to believe in.

"At first we listened, because we knew they were trying to protect us," Phyllis reflects on the Siberian Baptists' reluctance to evangelize outside the church walls. "But after a while, we realized it was deeper than that."

A strong sense of traditionalism (common among

Russian Baptists) had something to do with it—the kind of traditionalism that expects sinners wishing to repent to come to the church, not the other way around. Such a perspective wasn't unusual in Southern Baptist churches of days gone by, or even today in some places.

But the Hardies began to realize something even more basic. They were working with believers deeply shaped by generations of persecution—far more deeply than any outsider who hasn't experienced such trials can fully understand.

Remember, Novosibirsk was a city of exile in communist times. Prisoners and *undesirables* were sent there by the thousands: Jews, Germans, intellectuals—and evangelical Christians. And their trials did not end when they arrived. Many pastors and other Christians suffered martyrdom at the hands of Stalin's executioners. Children of believers were viciously abused and ridiculed in schools, or expelled altogether. Outcast and hated, denied jobs and shelter, Christian families constantly struggled to stave off hunger.

In a small city east of Novosibirsk lives a woman whose husband, a farmer, opposed the communist government. She had eight children. The communists killed her husband. They took the food from her garden and the family's cow and chickens, and left the woman to survive with eight children. She survived, and later became a part of the Baptist church there.

"It's people like that who make up the old brothers and sisters of the Baptist church in Novosibirsk," Charles explains. "When we got there we were not aware of just how much they had suffered. Many of the Baptists were very severely punished in the days of communism. And the Russian Orthodox Church strongly considered them a cult of the worst kind."

Christians enduring decades of such suffering developed what they called the "inner life" of the church: a very tight, controlled system of fellowship geared first to ensure survival, then to ward off the infiltration or attacks of communist agents and other potential persecutors.

Communist persecution may be gone for the moment. But for the Christian families that suffered so long from it, Charles observes, "it's very difficult to reach out and relate to the non-believer because of the fear. Too many old memories come back."

Adds Phyllis, "They're also very insecure. They're not sure that freedom is going to continue."

And they have reason to be concerned. Russia remains unstable, and widespread hostility continues toward "foreign cults"—encouraged by some politicians as well as the Russian Orthodox Church. Baptists often are lumped into that category, even though they have been worshipping on Russian soil for more than a century. New laws once again limit non-Orthodox religious groups.

So when the Hardies brought some of their new converts to the three Baptist churches of Novosibirsk, the leadership at first refused to accept them. These upstart believers had no family connection to the churches; they shared no heritage of suffering for the faith.

The breach grew so serious that at one point the Baptist leaders "did not want to continue to work with us," Charles relates. "The president of the Baptist Union suggested that we move to another city 10 hours by train east of Novosibirsk. I strongly felt before the Lord that it would be very ineffective to uproot and 'reroot' in a two-year period. We would lose a lot of ground."

Instead, after much prayer, the Hardies agreed to follow a set of rules laid out by the Baptists. Whenever Charles purposed to start a church, bring in new missions workers, or launch some other initiative, he would have to seek the approval of local church leaders.

"They had me go before the church to say that I would be willing to do that, and we are able now to work together in church planting," Charles says. "We still differ about some of these rules, but we can find common ground to work together. It's been difficult, but God has worked it out."

A Lost Generation Finds Jesus

Meanwhile, God was working all along through the Hardies' patient Bible studies—and their youthful colleagues' outreach—to begin several churches in the area.

One of them is a new congregation in an area called Chemskoi, home to about 60,000 people and not a single church—until now. Mama Pana, a Christian woman in her seventies, lives there. For years she went to one of the established Baptist churches in

Singing around the piano at Chemskoi Church

Novosibirsk, but that meant hours of commuting by bus and walking through ice and snow. Mama Pana sadly gave up the trek when her health started to fail. But she missed church and prayed for months that God would plant a church in Chemskoi.

The answer to her prayer came when someone asked the Hardies to begin a Bible study in the local children's center. Valentina, Mama Pana's daughter, directs the center. The Hardies began the study with five people. A little more than two years later, it had grown into a church with 50 adults and 15 children.

One of the first converts was Valentina herself. After several months of coming each week to the study, she asked to meet alone with Phyllis for counsel. She had a relationship problem with her sister that was causing great pain.

"As I shared principles and Scriptures for dealing with relationships, Valentina began to sob," Phyllis remembers. "She began to see the need of Christ in her life and as we prayed that night, she put her trust in Him."

Today Valentina unashamedly shares Christ with

teachers, children, and anyone else. "I wish I had a hook and could hook it into everyone to bring them to Christ," she declared one day. "We must hit this area and hit it hard with the gospel. There are lots of alcoholics and drugs here."

Another shining new beacon of faith is Irena, a woman in her early 30s and one of Charles' first language teachers. She began to ask questions about God. Irena came to their home to teach, and became good friends with Phyllis. The Hardies were the first Christians she had ever met.

Mama Pana

One day as Irena and Phyllis walked through the snow to shop, Irena asked a question: "You are so very far from your family and especially your daughters. I know it is very difficult to live in Russia, so how do you handle all these things?"

"Prayer," Phyllis answered. "Irena, people are praying for us. When I'm homesick, I just tell the Lord about it because He cares about everything in our lives."

"Phyllis, when you and Charles pray, I feel your prayers are reaching God," said Irena.

Throughout one summer, Irena indirectly shared the gospel over and over as she served as an interpreter for visiting Southern Baptist volunteer groups.

"One time as I was interpreting for a teenager to pray

and receive Christ, I made this prayer mine," Irena reflects. "I knew something had happened in my heart."

Irena really blossomed spiritually when she led her grandmother to Christ. This grandmother, who had rejected Irena for years, became quite ill. Irena knew her grandmother would not listen to her, but might listen to Irena's father. She asked her father to be her "translator" as she talked with her grandmother. He was reluctant, but finally agreed.

Irena, one of Charles' first language teachers and Phyllis' good friend

When her grandmother awakened from a coma, Irena shared the gospel. When she finished, her grandmother began to say, "I'm dirty. I'm dirty." They thought she was referring to her clothes or sheets, and assured her everything was clean.

She said, "No, you don't understand. I'm dirty. Jesus, save me. Jesus, save me!" She began to apologize to Irena's mother, whom she had disliked for many years. Then she went back into the coma and within hours died.

"Misha," 18, came out of a background of drug, alcohol abuse, and crime.

"He befriended us," says Todd Nance. "He was a very generous person in the first place. But once he came to faith in Christ, it was really neat to see him living life away from the drugs, away from crime, and working in some of the really poor neighborhoods, taking a leadership role sharing the Lord."

This onetime criminal-in-training, now a worship leader at the Chemskoi church, also says, "I cannot imagine my life without Christ."

"What has blessed us is this," Phyllis says. "We have not put legalistic burdens on these people but have loved, accepted, and prayed for them, and taught the Bible to them. The Holy Spirit reveals to them what their actions should and should not be. We have tried to communicate by our lives to love Jesus with all your heart and allow Him to be the motivator of your life, relationships, and desires."

Even some the most traditional Siberian Baptists are beginning to see how the Lord is moving. After questioning six of the new believers for two hours about their faith, Baptist leaders agreed to baptize them.

"You don't worship like we do, and you don't follow the same traditions," one of the leaders said. "But we can't find anything you're doing that is offending the gospel."

What's more, some of the children and grandchildren of older Baptists—not as scarred by memories of persecution—are joining the missionaries in more aggressive evangelism. One summer Sunday afternoon about 20 young people from Salvation Baptist Church, the largest of the older churches, came to sing at one of the new church starts. They set up speakers and microphones on the grass outside and sang and shared the gospel for about 100 listeners.

Russia may or may not gain real stability and prosperity in the days to come. But Charles and Phyllis Hardie are in Novosibirsk to stay

Charles baptizes new believers.

27

during their voluntary exile for the Lord. Why? When they were seriously considering moving during the toughest days, Irena came to them and said, "You can't leave us! We're baby Christians and we are watching your life to know how to walk with Jesus." That sealed their decision to stick it out.

Luke 10:1 says, "The Lord now chose seventy other disciples and sent them on ahead in pairs to all the towns and villages he planned to visit later."

"I believe God brought Charles and Phyllis to Siberia because He was already at work there in the hearts and lives of His people and in the hearts and lives of those He was preparing to receive Him," says missionary colleague Jack Shelby. "The abundant harvest they have seen thus far demonstrates this. I believe He is going to use them to open up new avenues for the gospel all over Siberia."

Phyllis leads a women's Bible study.

The Power of Commitment

Dewey and Bobbie Dunn in Venezuela

Dewey and Bobbie Dunn—two people passionately dedicated to God's purposes—reveal the potential of volunteer missions.

The crowd outside the building being used for a medical clinic was tired, increasingly unruly—and potentially dangerous.

Many of these residents of a poor barrio in a city of Venezuela had been waiting since long before dawn to see one of the North American medical volunteers inside. The number of people swarming around the Baptist-sponsored clinic had been doubled by an ongoing Venezuelan doctors' strike.

It was the last day of the clinic. The sun bore down on exhausted, expectant men, women, and children. It was becoming obvious that not everyone could be treated with the time and supplies left. Some patients had received donated eyeglasses out of turn, angering others who had been accidentally passed over. Venezuelan Baptist volunteers nervously circulated through the crowd, trying to keep order and prevent a riot.

As tensions climbed, a gringo emerged from the clinic door. He wore a long mustache and a baseball cap with a "V" (for Venezuela) on it. He looked as tired as the rest of the crowd, if not more so, after five days of near-nonstop doctoring. Accompanied by a Southern Baptist missionary

Bobbie Dunn fellowships with Venezuelan Baptist volunteers.

and the Venezuelan Baptist director of the clinic project, he made his way across the street to a basketball court where several hundred people awaited medical treatment.

He held up his hands, asking for a moment to speak, and the people grew quiet. Then he introduced himself: Dewey Dunn, a physician from Nashville, Tennessee, USA. He had been to Venezuela many times to treat the sick, and intended to come back as often as possible. He knew there was great physical need and suffering here.

"This is our last day to work here during this project, and we're going to do everything we possibly can today, but there are limitations," he told the crowd. "We've only brought so much medicine and so many eyeglasses. We're not going to take any of it back to the United States, but we're not going to be able to see everybody who is here today.

"We came here because God has blessed us in a wonderful way and we want to use what He has given us to bless people here. If we can see you, we thank God. If we can't, it's not because we don't love you and care about you. It's because we have done all we can do for now. We want you to know that God loves you, and we want to pray for you."

Silence descended over the chaotic place, and a Venezuelan led a short prayer. When it was over, he turned with his coworkers to return to the clinic. As they walked across the street, people began to clap and cheer—even those who didn't know if they would receive treatment that day. They sensed they had encountered a man who really cared about them, who was willing to work to the limits of endurance to demonstrate that care.

They also sensed the love of God and servanthood of Christ, not only in Dunn but also in the other Southern Baptist health volunteers, the missionaries aiding them, and the Venezuelan Baptists serving sunup to sundown as coworkers, helpers, and spiritual counselors. Of 2,100 patients treated by Dunn's team during the week, more than 500 people accepted Christ as Savior. That was only one of six volunteer teams in action in Venezuela during this early 1997 trip—one of five such projects planned by

Dunn for that year alone in Venezuela, Poland, Costa Rica, and Chile.

Exhausting, Yes. Boring, No.

A volunteer health evangelism trip organized by Dewey Dunn and his wife, Bobbie, may be exhausting (some volunteers jokingly call it being "Dunn in"), but it is never boring.

While Dunn and his colleagues headed off a potential riot during the project, his dental team barely averted being shut down by Venezuelan authorities. Someone had failed to obtain proper written permission or clearance, local health inspectors informed the team; they would have to cease work immediately.

But then the inspectors were invited to see what the team was doing. They were so impressed that they not only allowed the team to continue its ministry, but sent a dental chair, light, sterilization unit, and other equipment—a permanent gift to Venezuelan Baptists for use at

Dewey and Bobbie Dunn share the love of Christ as they minister to the physical needs of those they encounter.

the clinic and in future projects.

"I was frustrated at first because we were so busy," Dewey admits. "But without that interruption, we wouldn't have had those gifts given to Baptist work that the Lord will use in a wonderful way. That's just an example of how the Lord continues to teach us what He is doing when we face some adversity."

Difficulties included, Dewey came home saying the project was the "best ever."

"He always says it's the best ever," confides Bobbie— until the next one surpasses it.

This particular project did not go unnoticed by Venezuelan opinion makers. The newspaper *La MaOana* featured a large front-page photo of volunteer doctor George Oden examining a small child, with an enthusiastic story and more photos on the next page.

Southern Baptist volunteers meet medical needs "for the love of Christ."

"Owing to the runaway crisis in all areas of our society, various religious groups have realized the need to set aside their usual task of preaching in order to offer a different kind of service to our forsaken fellow man," the newspaper reported.

"That's the reason (the Baptists and US volunteers) are treating more than 6,000 people in the counties where the medical project has had the opportunity to set up clinics. . . ."

"With the love of Christ as a priority, the volunteers came here to offer health care. . . . Many children with parasites were treated. Dizziness, coughing, headaches, and leg pain were relieved with free medications. Most of the resources were donated by Baptist churches. . . . That these medical specialists should leave their homes and take part of their vacation time to work here or in some other part of the world in order to help a neighbor in need, for the love of Christ, is highly commendable."

Spiritual Crisis, Spiritual Answers

The "runaway crisis" identified by *La MaOana* reflects problems affecting Venezuela and other South American countries: poverty, social and political instability, economic turmoil. Venezuela's poor suffer many of the same physical ills afflicting the poor worldwide: parasites, gastrointestinal problems (Dewey's speciality), respiratory infections, and malnutrition.

But at a deeper level, Venezuela needs Jesus Christ. National health officials have acknowledged as much. During a 1993 visit to the government's Ministry of Health, officials "told us that the physical needs were great, but the spiritual needs were more important," Dewey recalls. "The Ministry of Health has given us complete approval to do these projects as we come to work in partnership with Venezuelans."

Partnership is the key word for each health project. Evangelism and church-starting are the objectives. The early 1997 project, for instance, focused two teams on strengthening new mission churches in Caracas while four teams served in the state of Falcón.

"It advances the work much more quickly in an area," Dewey says of the health care outreach. Baptists and mis-sionaries "get a boost. Extra help comes in and gives them a thrust forward. Health care teams come and then, in the same year, evangelism teams come and follow up and do house-to-house witnessing." The evangelism volunteers consolidate and build on the decisions made for Christ during the health clinics—setting the stage for planting churches.

This pattern of health projects followed by evangelistic campaigns is the heart of "Open New Works 2000," Venezuelan Baptists' national church-starting plan. Its first three-year phase launched 28 mission churches in and around Caracas.

Seeds of Commitment

The seeds of Dewey and Bobbie Dunn's continuing commitment to Venezuela were planted decades ago and farther north—in Guatemala. The Dunns, who met at Louisiana College, married following Dewey's first year in medical school. They visited Guatemala, where the young med student did research in pathology for several months. They also got a taste of missions there, thanks in part to Southern Baptist missionaries Clark and Sarah Scanlon. Clark became a mentor to Dewey, and took him around Guatemala to see missions in action.

Dewey and missionary Butch Strickland lead volunteers in singing and prayer before they leave for a day at the clinic.

Back in the United States, Dewey completed his medical training in several locations, including New York City, where he worked as an intern at the famed Bellevue Hospital. The Dunns also experienced missions in America as members of Manhattan Baptist Church. Medical service in the military followed, and work at the Veterans Administration Hospital in Kansas City. Dewey moved to Nashville in 1971 to teach at Vanderbilt University's medical school. He also joined the staff of the Veterans Administration Hospital in Nashville, where he would later become chief of gastroenterology.

The Dunns joined Woodmont Baptist Church in Nashville, which, interestingly enough, provided a home in 1976 for a missionary couple on furlough: Clark and Sarah Scanlon. Earlier that year a devastating earthquake had struck Guatemala. Clark led 30 volunteers from Woodmont—including Dewey—to the Central American nation to help it dig out and rebuild.

"That just turned our church upside down for missions," Dewey remembers.

It turned the Dunns upside down, too. Dewey joined another disaster relief team in the Dominican Republic after a hurricane there. He served the Wallace Memorial Baptist Hospital in South Korea. In 1987, after Tennessee Baptists began a missions partnership with Venezuela Baptists, the Dunns went with a volunteer evangelistic team to the South American nation. That visit began their love affair with Venezuela, which continues to this day.

The first project coordinated by Dewey brought no fewer than 175 health volunteers to Venezuela in 1988. Since then dozens of clinics have been held in cities, small towns, schools, churches, government facilities, homes, community centers, in the open air—even in a barn. Thousands of Venezuelans have met Christ in these places.

Tennessee Baptists moved on to partnerships with the Philippines, Chile, Poland, and Costa Rica. The Dunns have participated in all of these, but they keep going back to Venezuela. They love the country, its people, and working with the Southern Baptist missionaries and

Baptists who proclaim Christ there.

As in any relationship, there have been rough patches—particularly in the early days, as missionaries struggled to find places of effective service for the throngs of volunteers Dewey eagerly recruited. But the partnership has bloomed over the years. Now missionaries and Venezuelans accustomed to working with the Dunns' teams have become skilled health volunteers in their own right. In some areas Venezuelan Baptist health professionals now regularly initiate their own medical evangelism projects. It all focuses on these simple goals: loving and healing people as Jesus did, proclaiming His name, and starting churches.

"They do three things for us," explains missionary Butch Strickland of the health projects. "They give us an identity, they help people feel good for awhile, and they win a lot of people to the Lord in the communities where we work. A lot of Venezuelans don't know who Baptists are. To show them we desire to serve them gives us a tremendous identity.

"Some of the health care professionals who come down here wonder what good they're doing if they only give people a shot or a pill, and the health problems come back after a month. But that's an effective ministry. Maybe for one month out of their whole life, these people feel good. My job is church planter, and in the time I've been down here we've started eight churches. In every one, there are people who say, 'Yeah, I remember you guys. You did the medical project. I remember how good I felt when the doctors were here helping us.'"

Life-Changing Experiences

The early 1997 project brought 74 Southern Baptist volunteers from 12 states to Venezuela—doctors, dentists, dental hygienists, pharmacists, nurses, lab techs, physical therapists, optometrists, ophthalmologists, and non-medical helpers. At least half of the team members had been to Venezuela with the Dunns before—some many times. Here are the experiences of several:

"This was my second trip to Venezuela," says dental hygienist Ginger Brown of Tennessee. "As I watched God's hand in providing us with a dental chair, dental lighting, and autoclave [through the government inspectors], I stood amazed at His handiwork.

As Tennessee dentist Ken Mattox worked on patients, he watched as a 15-year-old Venezuelan Baptist volunteer counselor won 16 people to Christ, one by one.

"This trip has changed my life completely," says Linda Mills, a member of one of the "eye teams." The most powerful impression: seeing people declare their faith in Christ with great joy. "In El Nogal we gave a pair of glasses to a little lady, who kept reading the tract we gave her to look at. Then she would stop, lift her hands to the sky praising the Lord, and continue reading again. The Venezuelan people have my heart, and I have a much greater appreciation for the missionaries than before. God is good!"

Helper Steve Booth of North Carolina, on his fourth trip, visited a church he helped build three years before—now filled with people and the Spirit of God "from one end to the other. Even though I don't have a medical background, this trip was hard work . . . but with overwhelming pay—the salvation of many, many people."

For Dewey Dunn himself, the sheer multitude of patients during this latest "best trip ever" stood out—along with the number of people meeting the Lord. For his team alone, "there were three days with over 100 decisions for Christ, and on the last day I was personally blessed to have six people receive Christ at my desk." For Bobbie, who often works with the eye teams, the highlight was a tiny woman who walked into the clinic and sat in a corner with no expression. When Bobbie found a pair of eyeglasses that helped her, "her whole countenance changed. She smiled. She came to life again. It's those kinds of experiences that make all the old dirty glasses worth washing."

Pharmacist Larry Poston of Tennessee was another repeat volunteer—returning for his 16th time! Why? Let him explain: "The greatest pleasure a Christian can enjoy is the joy of salvation. The second is to feel you are fulfilling God's purpose for your life. These trips give me the feeling that I am within His will, and they charge me up for deeper commitment and added service."

Not everyone is a repeat volunteer, of course. Dewey delights in persuading folks who've never even stepped on an airplane to embark on an international missions adventure. He pairs them with veteran volunteers who show them the ropes and help them discover the joy of service.

After repeated invitations from Dewey over several years, dentist Ben Locke and his wife, Lucy, took their first missions trip on their 25th wedding anniversary in 1996. They traded a romantic getaway for long, hot days pulling teeth and filling cavities. While Ben worked on patients, Lucy held a flashlight to help him see inside mouths, rubbed his aching back, wiped his brow, and told patients about Jesus.

"The trip turned out to be very good for our marriage," Lucy insists. "Even though I know Ben works very hard and cares about his everyday patients, it was really

**Dewey and all the volunteers work from early morning
to late afternoon helping those who wait in long lines.**

special for me to see how he cared so deeply for the Venezuelans"—and to see more than half of the 3,000 patients treated by their health teams make decisions for Christ. "I can't wait for the next trip."

Ben agrees: "Seeing (Lucy) serve others in Christ's name moved my love for her to the next level."

On the other end of the marriage spectrum, a newly-wed couple spent their honeymoon on the same project. In addition to starting their life together by serving God, the young couple had the joy of meeting other volunteers like 84-year-old physician Gib Kelly, on his 11th trip, who has continued participating in projects even after the amputation of one of his legs.

Taking the First Step

One reason why so many volunteers return again and again: Dewey Dunn has a remarkable gift for getting Southern Baptist health professionals hooked on volunteer missions. He considers it his calling from God to encourage Christian health workers to use their lives and talents for Christ in missions. That involves taking a step beyond our own resources, out of our comfort zone, he explains, and becoming "God-reliant" rather than self-reliant. Then one can develop what Dewey calls a missions lifestyle.

The challenge comes in getting people—especially doctors, a self-reliant group if there ever was one—to take that first step: a volunteer trip. Easier said than done. For Dewey, recruiting for a project means endless hours of prayer, making contacts, encouraging participation, and gently challenging busy professionals to make time. Gently like a bulldog, says one close friend and medical colleague. But that's what it takes.

"People have so many other priorities," admits Alabama physician Jerry Graham, who held out as long as he could before going to Venezuela with the Dunns. "I'm not critical of them because I was just as guilty. I said no for many years until I finally said yes. It was Dr. Dunn's loving persistence—not just persistence, but loving persistence."

Sometimes loving persistence is persistent indeed, as Clark Scanlon illustrates:

"When Dewey gets up one of these 150-person teams, he may call an orthopedic surgeon and say, 'Look, I really need an orthopedic surgeon for this trip. It's a tremendous opportunity. I know how much money you make, so don't tell me you can't afford it or you're too busy. You're no busier than I am, so get somebody to cover for you and come down with us.' Only a highly competent peer could talk like that. But they respond."

Some have not only responded, but gone on to missions projects in other countries. Some have become career medical missionaries through the International Mission Board.

As another frequent volunteer doctor observes, it's hard to get mad at a guy who walks the talk, who is completely dedicated to a cause. It's also hard to say no to him. He's not known for being a great speaker or a charismatic leader, but he moves people by his utter sincerity. His intensity and passion for medical missions are contagious.

The Action Never Stops

The action never stops, even at home. With an average of three to five mission trips a year, Dewey and Bobbie are always preparing for, participating in, or recovering (quickly) from a project. His position as chief of gastroenterology at the VA Hospital is more demanding than ever as the hospital staff and patient load has grown. But it also gives him extra flexibility; not owning a private practice, he doesn't have to shut it down when he heads overseas.

Vacations? "Dewey doesn't take vacations," Bobbie states. Missions is more fun—and fulfilling.

A typical day in Nashville finds Dewey working at the hospital, perhaps at Woodmont talking missions, then at home on the phone—often late at night—enlisting volunteers for the next project. "I can't even begin to imagine what his phone bill is," says one medical colleague.

When he attends annual meetings of the Baptist Medical-Dental Fellowship, he doesn't sit around and shoot the breeze with colleagues; he mans his own information booth to recruit health professionals for missions. The fruit of such efforts: a network of hundreds of regular volunteers, regularly replenished by new blood.

Beside him at every step is Bobbie.

"She is the ballast; the calm; the enabling, foot-slogger infantry that keeps Dewey soaring," says Clark Scanlon. At home she juggles a thousand details in project preparation that Dewey lacks the time to chase down. On the field, she often leads one of the eye teams ministering to patients. Even a struggle in recent years with lymphoma hasn't stopped her, although medical treatment has slowed her down.

"Who do you think does the groundwork?" asks Bobbie's friend and frequent volunteer Virginia George, a retired professor of nursing. "Who do you think takes all the faxes and answers the phone all day and gets the donated medicine out of the little sample packets? Their living room looks like the city dump when we're emptying medicine bottles to get ready for a trip."

Together, they are a powerful team. And they have no plans to stop as long as the Lord gives them the strength to serve.

"Dr. Dunn has one of the biggest hearts for missions of anybody I've ever met," says former missionary to Venezuela, Bill Cashion. Bill is now IMB Human Needs Director and he worked with the Dunns in Caracas. "When I think of him and Bobbie, I think of two people who sincerely love others because they sincerely love the Lord."

Wandering
with Nomads

Troy and Melissa Haas in Kenya

In the harsh desert home of Kenya's Turkana people, Troy and Melissa Haas intend to spread the gospel—whatever it takes.

The blacktop road from Nairobi, a 12-hour drive, winds its way down ancient African slopes to the floor of the Great Rift Valley. It toils across a yawning expanse of desert, and ends at the town of Lodwar in Kenya's far northwest.

Surrounding the town: a moonscape of scrubland, rock, thorns, and sand—scorched by the sun, blasted by an endless oven wind, whipped by sandstorms that turn sunlight strange shades of orange.

This is the homeland of the Turkana people, who wander its vastness in search of water and grazing for their goats and camels. Bordered by Uganda, Sudan, Ethiopia, and huge Lake Turkana, it covers more than 23,000 square miles.

You can't live out there, Kenyans warn any outsiders rash enough to consider it. Even the proud Turkana, who've led a nomadic existence in the region for centuries, have struggled to survive the merciless droughts of recent decades.

"I admire them," says Southern Baptist missionary Jill Branyon, who works elsewhere in Kenya but actively prays for the Turkana and recruits others to do the same. "I couldn't survive 10 minutes out there. Yet they do it as a matter of course."

During one visit to the region, Jill went out into the bush with some experienced missionary guides. There she got a glimpse of the Turkana genius for survival.

"We drove out a long way to an area where they wanted to start work," Jill relates. "We went to a riverbed and this little Turkana girl scooped water out. It was just swirling with mud. I thought, 'She can't drink that. What's she going to do with it?' She went over to a certain tree, cut off a piece of root and flayed it open like a paintbrush. Then she swirled that muddy water and all the mud went immediately to the bottom. The top was almost clear. I still wasn't interested in drinking it, but it was vastly different from the water she had pulled out of the river. There also was a little boy who had built a bird trap, and the complexity of the levers and pulleys he used just floored me. These people are brilliant, and I was enthralled with them."

Some Turkana have adopted settled lives in Lodwar and other towns, either to escape the threat of death by drought or the sheer harshness of their traditional existence. Others have gathered in agricultural or fishing settlements along the shores of Lake Turkana.

Some of these settlers have responded enthusiastically to the gospel, thanks to the faithful efforts of missionaries and Kenyan Christians. But the town dwellers comprise only about 10 percent of the Turkana—who number more than 300,000—and they have essentially abandoned traditional nomadic Turkana culture. Drive 30 minutes outside of Lodwar, and you can find Turkana families who've never been to any town—and never heard of Jesus.

**Most of the Turkana are nomads
wandering the desert lands of northern Kenya.**

"Western missionaries who have gone to evangelize the Turkana are effective largely among settled groups," reports one missions profile. "The nomadic way of life is too difficult for most of them," or even for other Kenyans. As a result, concludes another report, "a truly effective (evangelism) strategy that speaks to the Turkana has yet to be discovered."

Troy and Melissa Haas propose to discover one.

On the Edge

The Haases, a young Southern Baptist missionary couple from Texas, have a small house in Lodwar they visit on weekends. It has modern conveniences like electricity (more often than not) and running water. There they can take a break, enjoy the cool breeze from a fan, make phone calls, and check email.

But most days find them—and their daughter, Rachel, born in 1996—living in a tiny thatched hut out in Turkana country. Even that is more settled than they plan to be during their next term of service. Once they have mastered the Turkana language,

Troy and Enok, his language assistant, talk to young women from the village who have come to visit. They are sitting in front of the Haases' hut.

they hope to begin traveling with nomadic Turkana clans, moving whenever the clan moves. They can load everything they need to live into (or on top of) their Nissan Patrol.

"We look like the Beverly Hillbillies when we drive out," Melissa jokes.

What makes a couple of middle-class, Generation X Americans raised on fast food and television think they can succeed in such an experiment? Why would they even want to try when other missionaries have failed?

"Troy is hardheaded," says Sam Turner, the veteran Kenya missionary who gave them the go-ahead to attempt it. "And Melissa is a real jewel."

Determination will help, but here's the motivation: The Turkana people need to hear about Jesus, and the Haases believe God wants them to deliver the message. Without His grace, they know they have no chance to make it.

With it, they intend to help evangelize the Turkana.

Troy first experienced God's grace when an African reached across cultures to tell him about Christ. At the time, he was careening in the opposite direction.

"I got off on the bad side of things in high school— heavy drugs and lots of other stuff," Troy recalls. "I ended up in trouble with the law, and it's really a miracle that I'm not dead or in prison at this point. I was a student at Texas A&M University and a Nigerian exchange student shared the gospel with me for the first time in my life."

God sent others to lead Troy toward salvation, and led him to Sagemont Baptist Church in Houston, which has been his base of spiritual support ever since. He later baptized his own father there.

Troy dropped out of Texas A&M during his wild days, but as a growing young Christian he enrolled in East Texas Baptist University in Marshall with a sense of God's calling to full-time Christian work.

In school and church, in Baptist Student Union ministries, and later as a church staff member involved in youth ministry and evangelism, he poured the same energy into God's purposes that he had once applied to self-destruction.

"Troy always wanted to be on the edge, pushing the limits," observes one of his closest friends, John Guedry, a classmate in college and later at Southwestern Baptist Theological Seminary. John cites an example:

"He was always looking to be in the most challenging ministry at church. He's never lost sight of the fact that once he was the kind nobody was going to bother ministering to. He was just a dope smoker wreaking havoc on the streets, yet somebody spoke the power of the gospel to him at an eternally ordained moment. And he has never been the same."

Melissa's early days could hardly have been more different. She grew up in a strong Christian home, gave her life to Christ as a young girl, and never doubted His love and plan for her life while preparing to be a teacher. But she was drawn just as strongly as Troy toward the lost. She served as a Home Mission Board (now North American Mission Board) summer missionary twice, and committed herself to vocational mission service after her sophomore year in college.

Troy and Melissa had been friends for several years in college and Baptist Student Union. When they became prayer partners and later began dating, a potent missions team was born.

"Melissa has always been one of the most compassionate and reflective people I know," John adds. "Once she and Troy fell in love, they began to develop the same heart. Their theme once they began to look toward missions was always to go into an undeveloped or unreached area."

Would that be somewhere in the United States—or on an overseas missions field? Troy and Melissa didn't know. The question was premature, since they hadn't even decided whether to get married. Both questions were answered in one evening at the closing service of the "Missions '90" conference in Fort Worth, Texas.

"The last night of the conference, the Lord moved in my heart and I really felt called strongly to foreign missions," says Melissa. "I remember looking over to Troy while the Lord was dealing with me and thinking, 'Lord, what about him?' and the Lord said, 'You've

Melissa, Rachel, and Troy. Troy is holding a traditonal Turkana walking stick (an aburo) and an ekicholong, used both as a seat and a headrest.

got to trust Me and commit to Me first.' On the way home that night, Troy said, 'What did the Lord say to you?' I told him, and Troy said, 'Well, He said the same thing to me.'" They became engaged less than a month later.

Another critical encounter at "Missions '90": the excited young couple met Jimmie and Peggy Hooten, veteran Africa missionaries on a furlough from Kenya. They talked for three solid hours about God's call and missions.

While they were engaged, Troy and Melissa participated as volunteers in a major evangelistic crusade focusing on Kenya's heavily Muslim coastal city of Mombasa. The Hootens, meanwhile, returned to Kenya and their work among the Maasai people, traditional animists who had been coming to Christ by the thousands as a result of prayer and pioneer missions efforts.

"Lo and behold, we got a call in 1991 from Troy and Melissa in the United States," Jimmie remembers. "They had gotten married and were going to Switzerland for their honeymoon, and they said, 'Could we come on down and

Troy and a Turkana man sit on their ekicholongs (left). Through storying—passing along the stories of the Bible in an oral tradition—Troy and Melissa spead the gospel among the Turkana.

see y'all in Kenya, too?' We said sure. They came and stayed for five weeks! With Peggy and me out there in the middle of Maasai country, they just fell in love with it. Troy rode around with me, and they were troopers."

Two years later (Melissa had to wait until she reached age 24 to be appointed by the International Mission Board), the Haases returned to Kenya—as Southern Baptist missionaries assigned to the Maasai.

Over the Edge

As they pursued Swahili language study and prepared to work among the Maasai, however, Troy and Melissa grew restless. Some 100,000 Maasai had come to Christ during the 1980s, and the church among them was becoming well-established and self-sustaining. The Haases felt God nudging them toward people who had never heard the gospel.

A village in the Lomil area near the Sudan border. Troy talks to the men while Melissa talks to the women.

"The Lord said, 'I'm here and I have a witness here, and in 10 years this area will be reached. There is another place I need you more,'" Melissa recounts.

They prayed long and hard before approaching the Kenya Baptist Mission leadership about their spiritual struggle. "We were scared," Troy admits—scared of being rebuked as starry-eyed young upstarts asking to shirk their missions assignment before they had even begun. Unable to shake their sense of restlessness, however, they timidly asked to meet with Kenya missionary administrator Sam Turner.

Instead of rebuking them, Sam said, "I've been waiting for you to come for months." The missions organization—and Kenyan Baptists—had been praying for some time about sending missionaries to the Turkana and Boran peoples in northern Kenya. Living conditions were so difficult among both peoples, however, that missions and Baptist leaders refused to press anyone to take on the task without clear leading from God.

The Haases visited the areas inhabited by both peoples—and prayerfully chose the Turkana.

"The Turkana are where the Maasai were 10 to 15 years ago," explains Troy. "They are beginning to get ripe for the gospel. They are animists and very traditional. But the Boran are Muslim, a barrier which is going to take years of seed planting and relationship building to overcome. The Turkana work is ready now with a little bit of plowing. If you have a garden that's ready to harvest and

Some of the young Turkana women Melissa is trying to reach

you don't harvest it, the fruit will go bad."

Ongoing drought and social and political pressures also forced even the most nomadic Turkana to consider change—opening doors for the Lord to work in ways He couldn't work before.

"I think what happened among the Maasai is going to happen among the Turkana," Jimmie predicts. "Within five years there's going to be a breakout, and it will sweep other peoples as well. There are a bunch of unreached people groups in northern Kenya, northern Uganda, Ethiopia, and Sudan."

Into the Bush

The Haases moved to Lodwar in January 1995. They began by getting to know the town-dwelling Turkana people, including the members of several churches started by Kenyan Baptists. While studying Turkana culture and language, they worked with church people in basic discipleship training.

The transmission promptly dropped out of their first vehicle, a used model accustomed to easier days farther south. So they did plenty of walking around town. It slowed their transportation, but sped up the process of making friends.

They made their first trip into the bush in early 1996—carrying all the water and supplies they would need for two days—to the homeplace of William Ebenyo, a Turkana pastor in Lodwar. It was a fitting initiation into daily life with the Turkana: Melissa drank fresh camel's milk, gathered firewood with Turkana women, and made goat stew on an open fire. She even received a Turkana name: *Atabo*, the word for the place where Turkana sleep under the stars. Troy was named *Ekitoi*—tree.

Troy brought his *ekicholong*, a small wooden stool (also used as a pillow) that self-respecting Turkana men are never seen without. He was allowed to sit with the men for their favorite activities: swapping stories, talking about their prized animals, and drinking tea.

Troy and Enok (in pink striped shirt) talk to Joseph Ingolan (left), a Baptist pastor in Lodwar.

It was a friendly visit, but it didn't mean the Haases would be accepted. Turkana people are polite but reserved around newcomers—a caution bred by cultural tradition, hard times, and interference or attacks by outsiders.

"They'd be suspicious even of another Turkana they didn't know who popped into their area," Troy explains. "They are very individualistic and very untrusting of outsiders."

Piercing that wall of suspicion is crucial for anyone hoping to spread the gospel among the Turkana, for their society is based on the forging of personal friendships. Troy and Melissa labored for a year to initiate relationships in an area where another evangelical group offering help had basically been told "thanks but no thanks" by Turkana elders. The same smiling rejection could have stopped the Haases, but they were aided by a near-tragedy.

The brother of one of the Turkana leaders in the area was struck by a bus in Lodwar and left for dead. But like the Good Samaritan, the Haases got him medical care before it was too late and arranged for payment. That made a powerful impression on the grateful Turkana leader.

"We developed a strong friendship with this man, and through our friendship with him, we've gotten to know many of the other leaders in the community," says Troy.

He approaches their culture very respectfully. "I wear the same sort of things that they wear, I carry my little wooden stool and wooden cane that every Turkana man has. I have goats just like they have, and we try to live in a way that doesn't offend them. I guess what we try to do is not put any more 'offense' in the gospel than is already there [for unbelievers]. I don't need to add more stumbling blocks by being culturally insensitive."

One cultural approach that definitely does not offend the Turkana is storytelling. Like many peoples the world over, they relish stories and the art of passing them on around a meal or a fire.

Troy and Melissa hope to use Bible *storying* extensively with Turkana families. This increasingly popular missions method presents the great narrative stories of Scripture, beginning in Genesis and climaxing with the life and saving mission of Jesus Christ. The technique is particularly effective in primarily oral cultures like the Turkana.

The Turkana believe in one God, a distant Creator, but they don't understand who He is, or that He wants to have a personal relationship with them. How can Bible storying begin to communicate His nature to them? Troy relates an intriguing incident from his early efforts:

> I met an old Turkana man on one of our many trips to visit our friend Erot. He lives in an area that always has water and is a favorite place of Turkana to come in times of drought. I asked the old man, Lomosia, if I could be his friend, and he replied yes—if I proved my word was true by coming to visit him again within a month. Excited about the opportunity to build a relationship with another traditional Turkana family, I made plans to return in three weeks' time.
>
> When I arrived at his home, Lomosia was thrilled and called all the other elders in the community to gather and greet me. As the women were preparing tea, a rainstorm came up, and all of us men sat on our small stools and draped our blankets over our heads during the brief shower. Only a few minutes later, a beautiful rainbow appeared in the sky.
>
> Sensing the Holy Spirit's direction to use the rainbow as an opportunity for witness, I asked all the elders what the rainbow was called in the Turkana language. They replied *Ekipe*, which is literally translated *Satan*. I asked why, and they told me how Satan himself put this mark in

the sky to stop the rains that would make them able to survive and prosper. Breathing a prayer, I asked if I could share with them what God's Word says about the rainbow.

And so, for the first time in their lives, these Turkana elders heard a story from God's Word, the story of Noah and the ark, and how God hates sin but loves the people whom He has created. Their expressions were ones of enjoyment, then disbelief, then confusion. Was the rainbow a promise of love or a curse of hate?

The men were silent as I finished the story, and we went on to talk of other things. But I know that the first seed was planted in their hearts.

The Haases' goal before the end of their first term in Turkana country was to be able to tell a story well in the Turkana language.

Troy holds little Rachel in front of their hut.

They decided to spend most of their days in a Turkana hut south of Lodwar—partly to learn more about daily life, but mostly to concentrate on the critical task of learning the difficult Turkana language. Probably 90 percent of the Turkana know little or no Swahili, Kenya's main language.

The hut, about 150 square feet, is made of grass and palm leaf thatch with a wooden door and a dirt floor. Water comes from a hand-dug well in a riverbed a mile or so away. An outhouse stands about 150 yards from the hut. The Haases take sponge baths and mostly cook over an open fire. Concessions to modern technology: a two-way radio for communicating with other Kenya missionaries, a portable water filter, and an occasional meal cooked on a small stove.

The Haases' daughter, Rachel, was born near the end of 1996. Melissa spent the last few months of her pregnancy in Lodwar, and went to Nairobi to give birth. But when they got back to Turkana country, baby Rachel joined Mom and Dad in the hut. They cover her portable bed with a mosquito net to keep out spiders and scorpions. Outside, they protect her with a hat and sunscreen. Mother and daughter stay inside during the heat of the day.

Regarding various uninvited creatures, they follow the "old rule of the West: you shake out your blankets and shoes before you lie on them or put them on," Melissa cautions. "We've killed three scorpions and had visits from one snake, different spiders, a bat, and a little cute desert rat.

Troy and Melissa have given up amenities that we take for granted in order to share the good news of Christ with the Turkana. Melissa often cooks over an open fire.

The snake was nonpoisonous, and none of the scorpions are deadly. They just cause a lot of pain and discomfort."

She downplays suggestions of hardship or sacrifice. "A lot of it is just common sense; it's not too difficult. I asked the Lord to give me a real sense of flexibility. If I can make whatever I'm living in seem like home, then I'm fine. I just settle in. I'm a real nester. It's really what you decide you're able to live with. As long as I have water and that kind of thing, it doesn't bother me. As far as Rachel is concerned, she doesn't know any different, so she'll adjust better than any of us."

Troy, however, credits his wife for the success of the experiment so far. "Melissa is extremely mild mannered, calm, flexible, and patient. Not just any woman could do what we're doing. I am very thankful for the grace God has given to her. Whether we are in a tent or hut or whatever, if she can just have a few little things to make it kind of homey, she is perfectly content."

They both admit to having their bad days, when they long for a real bathroom, a little privacy from Turkana visitors who walk in "any old time," or solid walls and windows to keep out the sand that constantly blows through the thatch.

"You just learn to live with it," says Melissa.

Meanwhile, Rachel has helped Melissa in her mission of making friends among Turkana women.

"You're not considered a real woman until you've had a baby," Mom explains. "She's a real conversation opener. Most Turkana have never seen a white baby. The old men like to bless her. They hold her up in the air and sort of spit up and down her body. She has a Turkana name, *Achwa*, which means spring that never runs dry."

Daily life will grow much more challenging when they return from furlough back in the United States. That's when they'll attempt to travel with groups of Turkana in order to share the stories of the Bible effectively. Troy even hopes to add camels to his herd of goats.

"If we are discipling a certain group of folks and they move, we'll probably just pack up and move with them,"

Troy forecasts. "Remember, we're talking about an area the size of South Carolina. Being able to move around will extend our influence much more than being settled in one particular area."

They hope the Turkana they win to Christ will tell those Bible stories to others, touching off a chain reaction that will spread God's saving truth, family by family, through Turkana culture—and beyond.

The Turkana are one of a group of related tribes in Kenya, Uganda, Ethiopia, and Sudan called the Karamajong Cluster. They total more than a million people and speak similar dialects. Several of them are even more unreached by the gospel than the Turkana—especially in civil war-wracked Sudan, ruled by Muslim Arabs who brutally persecute Christians. Could all these peoples be evangelized in the days and years to come?

That dream is worth the price of any amount of inconvenience, the Haases believe.

"We're not doing anything other than what the Lord has called us to do," Troy insists. "If living like this makes it easier for the Turkana to hear and accept the gospel, then we are willing to do it. This is a wonderful place, because it is where God has told us to be."

Through God's eyes, the dry and weary land of the Turkana looks like Eden.

Conclusion

God is moving—with wonder-working power.

He is moving in places once ruled by tyrants. He is a shining light among entire people groups long enslaved by darkness. He is tearing down powerful spiritual strongholds and barriers built by hostile forces.

We've seen in this study how three couples are following God. A veteran missionary couple daring to enter a difficult new field just opened to missionaries. A volunteer pair dedicating virtually all their free time to medical evangelism projects. Two young missionaries willingly launching out into a dry, forbidding landscape to touch a tribe thirsty for the truth. What about you? Will you follow?

As never before, God's wonder-working power is opening doors of service for every Christian. Whether you're a high school student or a retiree, He may be calling you to serve as a volunteer. Teens, do you hear God asking you for your life as a career missionary, or for one or two years after college? Middle-agers, what about that meaningful second career you've restlessly searched for? Pastor and church family, how will you become a part of God's mission through targeted prayer war, through sending your best servants, through growing financial support?

God isn't waiting for us; He is moving. May we obediently follow—because we love Him—and lift His glorious name among the nations!